NOT-FOR-PARENTS

EUROPE
Everything you ever wanted to know

Clive Gifford

CONTENTS

NOT-FOR-PARENTS

THIS IS NOT A GUIDEBOOK. And it is definitely Not-for-parents.

IT IS THE REAL, INSIDE STORY about one of the world's most colorful continents—Europe. In this book you'll read about **bizarre** pastimes from **wok racing** and mobile phone hurling to grown-up food fights and **rotten shark chomping.**

You'll learn the gruesome facts about some of history's most **bloodthirsty** rulers and can check out sculptures made of **human bones**, the world's **biggest pizza**, **ultracool ice hotels**, and a metal-munching Frenchman.

This book shows you a **EUROPE** your parents probably don't even know about.

NATIONS OF EUROPE

Every nation in Europe has its own culture, traditions, and laws. And some are downright odd. It's illegal, for example, to feed pigeons in Venice, Italy, flush toilets after 10pm in Swiss apartments, or tune pianos at midnight in Germany. Neither can you name a pig Napoleon in France or build sandcastles on the beach at Eraclea in Italy.

Iceland

Short and Swede

While there is a place in northern France called Y, Norway and Sweden take the prize for having the shortest placenames. There are three different villages all called Å in the county of Troms in northern Norway, which must get confusing. Sweden has an Å of its own—and another village called Ö.

Ireland

Uni
King

WHAT A MOUTHFUL

The place with the longest name in Europe is in Wales, UK… [deep breath]…

Llanfairpwllgwyngyllgogerychwyrndrobwllllantysiliogogogoch

It means… [another deep breath]… "Saint Mary's Church in the hollow of the white hazel near a rapid whirlpool and the Church of St. Tysilio of the red cave."

Banding together

A whole bunch of European countries have grouped together to form the European Union. They share a number of laws and 17 of these countries all use the same money, the Euro. There were around 15.7 billion Euro banknotes in use at the start of 2013. That's a lot of dough.

Spain

Portugal

Name change
Istanbul was once called Constantinople and before that Byzantium. It's the capital city of Turkey and the only capital city that spans two continents. Its western side is in Europe but if you take a short ferry ride or cross a bridge over the Bosphorus, you'll find yourself in Asia.

Sweden

Finland

Norway

Denmark

Estonia

Latvia

Lithuania

Belarus

Russia

Netherlands

Poland

Ukraine

Belgium

Germany

Czech Republic

Luxembourg

Slovakia

Moldova

Liechtenstein

Austria

France

Hungary

Switzerland

Romania

Slovenia

Croatia

Monaco

San Marino

Italy

Bosnia and Herzegovinia

Serbia

Bulgaria

Andorra

Montenegro

Kosovo

Albania

Macedonia

Vatican City

Turkey

Greece

Cyprus

WANT MORE?

Check out the flags of Europe ☆ www.nationsonline.org/oneworld/flags_of_europe.htm

FOOD FIGHTS

Every kid loves a good food fight and it turns out quite a few adults in Europe do, too. Here are three messy festivals that prove the point.

COME ON, YOU'RE BEHIND. TRY TO KETCHUP!

Paint the town red

The sleepy town of Buñol near Valencia, in Spain, has a population of 9,000. But on the last Wednesday in August, numbers swell to five or six times that. All the visitors come for La Tomatina—the mother of all food fights.

A tomato thrower makes a splash in a slushy street.

Tomatoes are slightly acidic, which means they help to remove dirt. So once the streets are hosed down they are left sparkling clean.

Take that splat!

An hour before midday, giant trucks trundle into town and dump around 150,000 old tomatoes. Everyone grabs what they can and throws tomatoes into the crowd. That's 44 tons (40 tonnes) of tomatoes squished and squashed in just 60 minutes of mayhem. It's Tomatageddon!

Hip, hip, purée

An hour later a rocket fires to tell everyone the fun is over. The streets are left swimming in tomato slush, and friendly locals, along with firefighters, hose down the juicy revelers.

A JUICY BATTLE

The Battle of the Oranges in the Italian town of Ivrea started centuries ago and is said to commemorate the victory of villagers over an evil landowner. Today, around 3,000 people from the town do battle on foot or in horse-drawn carts. Many wear medieval clothing.

OF ALL THE WAYS TO GET MY DAILY DOSE OF VITAMIN C.

Messy meringue wars!
The Spanish town of Vilanova i La Geltrú is famous for *xató*—a salad of fish and vegetables. However, in February of each year, the diet isn't so healthy. As part of a festival, the townspeople hurl masses of meringues at each other. Other sweets are also thrown out into the crowds, which are packed with sweet-toothed kids.

Fruitful fight
Around 57,000 crates of oranges are shipped in for the Ivrea battle. These food fighters are serious! The end result is juice-soaked crowds and streets covered in pulp and peel.

WANT MORE?

Meringue Wars ☆ www.catalunyaonline.cat/carnavalvilanova/idioma_en.html

VLAD THE BAD

During the Middle Ages, there were many bad-boy rulers of kingdoms who thought nothing of slicing up rivals or plundering foreign villages and towns. But few were as brutal as Vlad III Dracul, also known as Vlad Tepes. Vlad was born into a powerful family. His father, Vlad II Dracul, ruled the kingdom of Wallachia (now in Romania) and was often at war with the mighty Ottoman Empire.

Vlad III Dracul

In 1442, when Vlad was 11, his dad sent him to the court of the Ottoman ruler, Murad II, as a hostage!

It's believed Vlad III had 20,000 to 100,000 people impaled on spikes!

It's a stick up!

Vlad III didn't like giving the enemy an honorable burial. Instead, he preferred to stick their dead heads on posts as a warning. Some victims were executed by being dropped onto sharpened stakes. This is how he got his nickname, Vlad the Impaler. During his reign, fields became full of impaled victims. Vlad even ate his dinner outside amid the grisly scenes.

WARRING WALLACHIA

Vlad III came to power in 1448 after his father was killed and rebels had blinded Mircea, his half-brother, with a red-hot poker, then buried him alive. Vlad's first spell in charge didn't last long but he returned in 1456 and ruled with an iron fist from his capital at Târgovişte.

Reign of terror

One legend tells that Vlad left a solid gold chalice or cup in the center of a public square for years. Anyone could have picked it up and stolen it—but no one dared to as the punishment for theft was, of course, death.

Hats off to Vlad

Many stories are told of Vlad III's cruelty. Once, foreign messengers visited his court in Târgovişte but refused to remove their hats. Angry Vlad had his guards nail their hats onto their heads.

Double ouch!

Vlad's head carved in stone

Watch your back

When he wasn't warring with the Ottomans, Vlad was wiping out rebellions and threats to his own power. He was imprisoned several times, and died in battle at the age of 45. The Ottomans carried Vlad's head back to Istanbul to reassure everyone that their arch enemy's deadly days were over.

Stoking the imagination

Bad Vlad's bloodthirsty ways, his birthplace of Transylvania and his name Dracul may have been the inspiration behind Bram Stoker's famous 1897 vampire tale, *Dracula*.

WANT MORE?

How were Vlad and Dracula different? ☆ www.vladtheimpaler.com

WHAT AN ICE PLACE TO VISIT

Deep inside the Arctic circle, 12 mi (20 km) from Sweden's most northern city, Kiruna, lies the village of Jukkasjärvi. In 1990, a French artist, Jannot Derid, held an art exhibition in a large igloo. One night, visitors couldn't find anywhere to stay. So they slept inside the icy igloo in sleeping bags laid on top of reindeer skins. A local businessman, Yngve Bergqvist, had a brainwave… what if we built a hotel out of ice?

The hotel bar is made from 44-55 tons (40-50 tonnes) of clear ice kept at -23°F (-5°C). Even the glasses and bowls are made from ice.

Hit hotel

As crazy as it sounds, the ice hotel was a huge hit and has been open for business ever since. Actually, a different hotel opens every summer because each one melts back into the nearby River Torne and has to be rebuilt.

Colorful drinks are served in glasses carved out of ice.

A subzero slumber room

Ice accommodation
Every year as winter comes, a large team of builders begin work. Blocks of ice from the River Torne are moved into place. Machines pump and spray snow onto frames to form rooms for more than 100 guests. The completed hotel features a large hall and reception area, a bar and even a church.

ARCTIC ART
Around 50 ice artists from all over the world descend on Jukkasjärvi. They begin work on the interior which includes ice chairs and tables, beds, and ornate walls. Ice is sawn, chiseled, and heated to form astonishing sculptures.

TOTALLY AWESOME!

Snow sights
You'll need a snowmobile, motorsled, or a sled pulled by husky dogs to take in the sights. The area is one of the best in Europe for viewing the astonishing northern lights, or aurora borealis, which appear in the night sky.

Aurora borealis

WANT MORE?

See and read more ☆ www.icehotel.com

A MEAL FOR A QUEEN

It's June 1889 and Italian cook Raffaele Esposito has a king-sized problem. King Umberto I and his wife, Queen Margherita di Savoia, are visiting Naples. Esposito has been invited to serve them dinner. Pizzas had only recently become popular, and it was said that the Queen had never tasted this simple dish before. Esposito was desperate to make her a special one.

King Umberto I

Margherita's a winner

According to legend, Esposito made three different pizzas. The one the Queen liked the most was topped with tomato slices, mozzarella cheese, and basil leaves to represent the red, white, and green of the Italian flag. The pizza, named in the Queen's honor, caught on in Naples and spread throughout Italy.

By Italian law, a real Margherita pizza must have thinly sliced San Marzano tomato, dough rested for six hours, and be cooked in a wood-fired oven.

PIZZA THE ACTION

The delights of Margherita pizzas spread to the United States via Italian immigrants and US soldiers returning home after World War II. Today, Americans eat more pizza than any other nation—three billion per year!

HELP, I'M MELTING...

YOU'RE SUPPOSED TO!

South Africa held the world record for the largest pizza until 2012, when five Italian chefs brought the record home with a 130-foot wide whopper (40 m)!

> **I KNOW I ORDERED THE EXTRA LARGE BUT THIS IS RIDICULOUS!**

Queen Margherita

GIANT PIZZA INGREDIENTS

4.4 tons (4 tonnes) tomato sauce
4.4 tons (4 tonnes) mozzarella cheese
419 pounds (190 kg) vegetable oil
1,488 pounds (675 kg) margarine
550 pounds (250 kg) sea salt
275 pounds (125 kg) Parmesan cheese

Germans top the Euro pizza-eating league, gobbling 275,000 tons (250,000 tonnes) of frozen pizza every year.

Spain
83,700 tons
(76,000 tonnes)

France
91,500 tons
(83,000 tonnes)

Germany
275,000 tons
(250,000 tonnes)

UK
165,000 tons
(150,000 tonnes)

FRESH & HOT IN 90 SECONDS!

Speedy pizza
This clever pizza vending machine makes a fresh pizza base from scratch, covers it in tomato sauce, and a choice of toppings, before baking it in less than two minutes!

WANT MORE?

The 130-foot pizza (40 m) weighed over 22 tons (20 tonnes) and took two days to bake!

In many parts of medieval Europe, if you weren't a 100% faithful follower of the Catholic Church, you'd better watch out. The Church was boss and anyone who opposed or practiced other faiths was a heretic. Inquisitions (organized church courts) questioned anyone suspected of heresy and punished those found guilty. These trials happened throughout medieval Europe and the most infamous was the Spanish Inquisition.

CONFESS OR DIE!

Isabella and Ferdinand

Worship warning

Set up in 1478 by King Ferdinand and Queen Isabella, the Spanish Inquisition was out to get you, especially if you were a Jew. Thousands of Jews were either punished or forced out of Spanish territory. Even good Catholics weren't safe.

Trial for heresy during the Spanish Inquisition

IS IT JUST ME OR IS IT HOT IN HERE?

RELAX!

Sentences varied from hefty fines or being whipped to life imprisonment or "relaxation." Although the last sentence was anything but relaxing—it meant you were burned at the stake. More than 2,000 people died this way in Spain.

GUYS, I'M NOT FEELING RELAXED YET!

Once you were 12, if a girl, or 14, if a boy, you could be interrogated by the Spanish Inquisition.

I DON'T BELIEVE IT!

Torturous ways

Some who denied doing anything wrong faced horrific torture. The Inquisition had a terrifying range of methods to make them confess. Each was more horrible than the last.

The water cure was pouring up to 14 pints (8 litres) of water through a cloth into someone's mouth to give the sensation of drowning.

ARE YOU PULLING MY LEG?

Bodies were stretched on the rack until bones snapped and joints dislocated.

An iron chain was tightened across the chest to cut into flesh. Thumbscrews (left) were tightened until thumb bones cracked.

THIS IS WHEELY UNPLEASANT...

Far from innocent

The first church leader to allow torture (in 1252) was named Innocent—Pope Innocent IV to be precise. Many torture victims confessed to things they hadn't done or died during torture.

A victim was lashed to a wheel which was then turned over a burning fire pit. They were slowly roasted to within an inch of their life.

WANT MORE?

Read more ☆ http://encyclopedia.kids.net.au/page/sp/Spanish_Inquisition

PET RESCUE

For more than 900 years, travelers through the treacherous Great St. Bernard Pass in Switzerland could find refuge in a small travelers' retreat. It was run by monks and called St. Bernard's Hospice. Dogs bred and kept by the monks became well known for their mountain rescues. This turned them into one of the most recognizable breeds of big pooches—the St. Bernard.

High-altitude route

The Great St. Bernard Pass allowed travel from Italy to France. Ancient Roman armies used it to invade Gaul (France) almost 2,000 years ago. In winter, the 49-mile-long pass (80 km) could be deadly. It had no trees for firewood or shelter and 33-foot-deep snow (10 m) in places.

Statue of St Bernard

EMPTY KEG

St. Bernard dogs are often pictured with a barrel of brandy around their necks. But it's a myth that they were ever worn. An 1820 painting by Edwin Landseer featured them and the idea caught on.

35 in (90 cm)

BIG BEASTS

St. Bernard dogs stand up to 35 inches (90 cm) tall at their shoulders. They have giant heads with powerful jaws. When they shake their heads, their great jowls can cover you in slobber…
URGH!

12 in (30 cm)

MIAOW!

THESE DOGS ARE PUSSYCATS!

Despite their size, these dogs are very friendly and gentle. They're the result of St. Bernard's Hospice monks breeding Swiss mountain dogs with other species of king-sized canines. They then trained the dogs to rescue lost or injured travelers.

The hospice was founded by Bernard of Menthon in around 1050. He was made a saint in 1681.

HOPE THEY'VE BROUGHT ME A TASTY BONE.

AH, PAW YOU! HERE, HAVE A SLOBBERY HUG.

More than 2,000 people's lives were saved by the dogs and monks. Outstanding!

Saved by slobber

The rescue dogs could sniff out a person trapped under many feet of snow. Whenever they found a victim, one would head back to alert humans. Meanwhile, one or more St. Bernards lay beside the casualty, keeping them warm and offering a friendly lick.

Well-kept pets

St. Bernard dogs last made a lifesaving rescue in the Alps in 1897. But dogs were bred and kept as pets at the hospice until 2004. Today, some of the dogs return to stay with the monks at the hospice during the summer.

90 HELVETIA

BIMILLENAIRE DU GRAND-SAINT-BERNARD
JULES-OLIVIER BERCHER 1989 COURVOISIER

WANT MORE?

Canine hero Barry (1800–1814) rescued more than 40 people on the pass.

LI'L LIECHTENSTEIN

Liechtenstein is bordered by Switzerland and Austria, and hasn't had an army or navy since 1868. Any serious criminal is imprisoned in Austria. There's no airport but it does have a postage stamp museum in a single room in the capital, Vaduz.

Country for rent
Since 2011, you can actually hire the entire country of Liechtenstein for $70,000 (£44,600) per night. For that you get your own personalized currency and street sign as well!

Independent: 1806
Area: 62 sq mi (160 sq km)
Population: 36,000

Liechtenstein is the world's leading producer of false teeth!

BLINK AND YOU'LL MISS 'EM

In Europe's long, long history, mighty empires have risen, fallen and disappeared from maps. Yet some small territories have survived. So, get out your atlas and magnifying glass to view the four tiniest nations of Europe. Known as micro-states, they are so small you could walk across two of them in less than half an hour and cycle across the others in 60 minutes max!

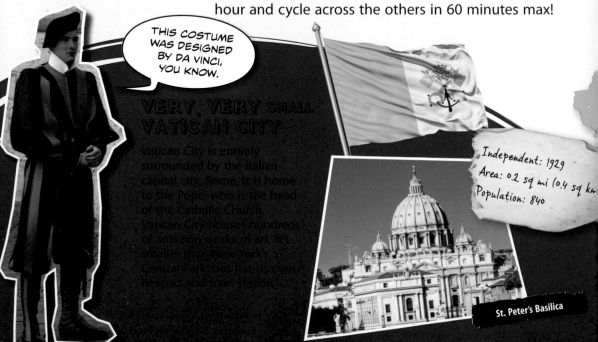

THIS COSTUME WAS DESIGNED BY DA VINCI, YOU KNOW.

VERY, VERY SMALL VATICAN CITY

Vatican City is entirely surrounded by the Italian capital city, Rome. It is home to the Pope, who is the head of the Catholic Church. Vatican City houses hundreds of amazing works of art. It's smaller than New York's Central Park, but has its own helipad and train station.

Independent: 1929
Area: 0.2 sq mi (0.4 sq km)
Population: 840

St. Peter's Basilica

MINUSCULE MONACO

Monaco is named after the monk's clothing Francesco Grimaldi wore the night he seized its fortress in 1297. Members of the Grimaldi family have ruled it ever since. Monaco's now home to many rich businesspeople and racing drivers, partly because they don't have to pay income taxes.

The Grotte de l'Observatoire in Monaco is the only cave in Europe where the temperature rises as you go deeper inside it.

Independent: 1297
Area: 0.8 sq mi (2 sq km)
Population: 36,400

Independent: 301 AD
Area: 24 sq mi (61 sq km)
Population: 32,400

SERIOUSLY SMALL SAN MARINO

San Marino is one of the oldest countries in the world. Surrounded by Italy, you can see the entire country from the top of its one peak, Mount Titano. Its Curiosity Museum includes a petrol-powered hairdryer, a watch to wear on your nose, and the world's biggest crab.

If that's not to your taste, how about San Marino's Museum of Torture with more than 100 medieval terror and torture devices?

I NEED A GET-OUT CLAWS!

WANT MORE?

Vatican City's cash machine instructions are in Latin.

BIG BANG

HOPE THIS SPARKS INTEREST IN MY STORY.

Alfred Nobel

On April 13, 1888, Swedish explosives maker Alfred Nobel (1833–1896) woke up, picked up a French newspaper and read that he had died. It was quite a shock. He felt perfectly fine. The newspaper had published Alfred's life story. It called him "a merchant of death" for inventing the powerful explosive, dynamite. Alfred vowed to do something to make people remember him more fondly.

Explosive ending
A chemist and engineer, Nobel was fascinated by explosives. He was particularly interested in nitroglycerine which was very unstable and could explode without warning. One such explosion killed Alfred's brother, Emil, in 1864. It left him determined to find ways to make nitroglycerine safer.

Nitroglycerine molecule

A dynamite idea
Nobel experimented with nitroglycerine on a barge in the middle of Lake Mälaren, Sweden. In 1866, he created a mixture of the explosive and a fine crumbly rock called *kieselgur*. It made a paste that could be shaped into rods which he called dynamite.

Just a bump could cause pure nitroglycerine to blow up.

Alfred Nobel

Where there's a will

Nobel died in 1896. In his will he left most of his fortune to give as prizes to people who made major advances in physics, chemistry, literature, peace, and medicine. A sixth prize in economics was added in 1969.

Prize money

The first Nobel Prizes were awarded in 1901. Wilhelm Röntgen of Germany won the first Nobel Prize for Physics for his discovery of X-rays. Today's winners receive a cool $1.2 million (£784,100).

Alfred Nobel created 355 inventions during his lifetime.

Nobel left more than 90% of his fortune to Nobel Prizes—about $305 million (£200 million) in today's money— a massive sum.

He set up about 90 factories around the world to make explosives.

In 1970, dynamite was used to blow up a dead sperm whale. Too much was used, resulting in chunks of whale flying 787 ft (240 m) and crushing parked cars!

WANT MORE?

More Nobel Prize facts ✫ www.nobelprize.org/nobel_prizes/nobelprize_facts.html

In 2002, six Moroccan border guards equipped with tents, a radio, and two flags "captured" Isla del Perejil from Spain. They renamed it Leila, but didn't stay for too long. A week later, Spanish forces recaptured the island without a struggle. It's not the only strange dispute over territory to occur in modern Europe.

I CLAIM THIS SUMMIT FOR ITALY!

MMM, STRANGE-TASTING GRASS!

Herb island
Isla del Perejil means Parsley Island in Spanish because that's what mainly grows on it. The island's only creatures are lizards, insects, and the occasional goat shipped over from Morocco to nibble on its plants and herbs.

STRANGE INVASIONS

Meet the royals
Here's Prince Roy and Princess Joan in 1966. Bow down to the mighty rulers of Sealand.

SEALAND
Britain built concrete sea forts to protect its coasts during World War II. All were torn down after the war except Fort Roughs Tower, in the North Sea. It lies about 7 mi (11.5 km) off the coast of England. In 1966, Roy Bates bought the sea fort, claiming it as a new nation called Sealand.

NON, NON, NON—
FOR FRANCE!

FEELING PEAKY

In 1861, Italy formed from a number of smaller states. At the time France and Italy agreed to share ownership of the highest mountain peak in the Alps— Mont Blanc. Sounds fine, except that some French maps have since been sneakily redrawn to show the peak inside France.

ROCKALL

This brilliantly named outcrop rises around 66 ft (20 m) above the north Atlantic Ocean. Rockall's ownership is challenged by four European powers: Iceland, Ireland, Denmark, and Britain. It's now up to the United Nations to settle the argument.

WHOOPS,
SORRY!

Lost In Liechtenstein
In 2007, 170 Swiss soldiers got lost during training and found themselves 0.9 mi (1.5 km) inside Liechtenstein. The Swiss quickly apologized for the accidental invasion. How polite!

I'M EGGS-
HAUSTED!!

In 2008, a team representing Sealand won the world egg-throwing championship!

Proud land
Other countries don't recognize Sealand as a real nation. But that hasn't stopped it from producing its own flag, stamps, and coins. For a small fee, you can even become a Lord or Baron of Sealand.

WANT
MORE?

Singer Ed Sheeran is a Baron of Sealand ☆ www.sealandgov.org/anouncements

THE FOOD, THE BAD, AND THE UGLY

Europe's a very civilized place, but that doesn't mean it can't get down and dirty when it comes to gruesome grub. Some strong-stomached Europeans swear by these delicacies, which would make a menacing menu if all served together.

OH, HAGGIS...!

Every year, on January 25th, Scots celebrate the birthday of their much-loved poet Robert Burns (1759-1796). They read out famous Burns' poems and eat haggis with mashed potatoes and turnips.

WHAT NOW...

Stinky shark meat
Never eat a freshly caught Greenland shark—it's poisonous! Icelanders get rid of the poison by gutting the shark then burying the body. Heavy stones placed on top squeeze the juices from the meat, which slowly rots for 2–3 months. The result? Hákarl—a tough, pinky-white meat which reeks of household bleach!

HMMMM... FEELING PECKISH?

WASTE NOT, WANT NOT

Meat's on the menu a lot in Europe, and few parts of an animal are wasted. In Iceland, the testicles of male sheep are boiled and then preserved in acid to make a strong-tasting dish. Minced-up sheep's heart, liver, and lungs (offal) are stuffed into a sheep's stomach (or large sausage skin) to make a haggis—the national dish of Scotland.

Haggis, mash, and turnips

Blutwurst (German)

Black pudding (English)

Morcilla (Spanish)

It's in the blood

In Germany, it's usually served cold and sliced. In England, it's often fried and eaten hot. What is it? The answer is sausage made mostly from the blood of pigs which has been left to congeal—turn from liquid to solid.

In some parts of Germany hot blutwurst served with potatoes is nicknamed *Tote Oma*, meaning "Dead Grandma"!

WHEEEE...!

Gooey maggot cheese

Casu Marzu is illegal to make but some sneaky Sardinians still do. This stinky sheep's milk cheese is left outside so cheese flies (Piophila casei) can lay their eggs in it. The eggs hatch into maggots, which wriggle through the cheese creating mushy goo. The cheese is eaten with the live maggots still inside.

Shut your eyes when you take a bite. The maggots can leap up to 6 in (15 cm) off the cheese!

WANTED

Casu Marzu Cheese

for crimes against good taste

WANT MORE?

In 2011, Lorne Coltart hurled a haggis 216 ft (66 m)—that's an offaly long way.

KNIGHT TIME

For centuries until the arrival of gunpowder, guns, and cannons, knights were the top dogs in medieval Europe. These armored men on horseback wowed women and awed men. Tournaments, where they displayed their skills, became colorful, exciting spectacles with battling by day and banqueting by night.

A jousting tournament on London Bridge, UK, watched by Richard II.

The Tourney

Tournaments began as good practice for battle but grew to provide other benefits. For lesser-known knights, they offered the chance of glory, building a reputation and being hired by a lord or king watching the spectacle.

I CAN'T SEE A THING IN HERE!

THUNDERING HOOVES

In a joust, the knights would charge at one another down a course 328–984 ft (100–300 m) long. They used a long wooden pole, called a lance, to try to unseat their opponent. It took great skill to gallop at speed while holding a shield and lance.

COMING TO GET YOU, READY OR NOT!

Bad luck

King Henry II of France was killed in a 1559 jousting tournament when nobleman Gabriel de Montgomery's lance pierced the visor of his helmet.

YIKES!

Prizes were often solid gold and worth more than a knight's yearly income.

A melée

THAT'S A GOOD KNIGHT OUT... OUCH!

I'M ONLY JOUSTING!

Fearsome free-for-all

The centerpiece of early tournaments was called a melée. This was a close-combat battle between knights on foot. Sometimes they were armed with wooden or blunted weapons. Judges would declare who won, while servants would carry away the dead and injured. They were kept very busy!

Protective metal gauntlets and helmet

WANNABE KNIGHT'S CHECKLIST

☐ Be born of noble blood (few peasants became knights).

☐ Leave home at 7 or 8 to live with a relative as a page (servant).

☐ Train hard to become strong and a good horserider.

☐ At 14–16, become a squire— a knight's apprentice.

☐ Work all hours to feed your knight and keep his armor clean.

☐ Learn to sharpen and handle weapons.

☐ At 20 or 21, convince a lord to dub you a knight.

Knight in shining armor

Knights originally wore suits of chain mail, made of up to 100,000 small, interlocking metal rings. By the 1400s, suits of heavy metal plate armor were usually worn. They weighed around 55 lb (25 kg). For jousting, the armor could weigh almost double that. Suits were reinforced on the side nearest their opponents—usually the left.

WANT MORE?

Jousts and tournaments ☆ **www.medievaleurope.mrdonn.org/jousts.html**

EAR WE GOGH

You can view more than 200 paintings by Vincent van Gogh (1853–1890) in Amsterdam, and hundreds more in France, Germany, and other European countries. Yet this amazing Dutch artist, who left behind more than 2,000 pieces of art, only painted for ten years. How did he manage such a feat, and why did he cut off his ear?

Van Gogh

This is one of 37 of Van Gogh's self-portraits.

Art life
Van Gogh was seriously bitten by the painting bug in his late twenties. He painted for days at a time, without food or sleep, until he was totally exhausted.

Early paintings, such as "The Potato Eaters," were dark and gloomy. But a move to Paris, in 1886, saw van Gogh's art lighten up.

Thick and fast
In Paris, van Gogh began piling on the bright colors and painting in quick, bold strokes. He was inspired by colorful Japanese art and the works of Impressionist painters.

WHAT'S FOR TEA?

IT'S POTATOES, THE SAME AS ALWAYS!

MY BACK'S KILLING ME!

SOLD *400 francs*

CAN WE MOVE YET?

WE'VE BEEN POSING FOR HOURS!

On sale
Van Gogh sold just one painting while alive. Called *The Red Vineyard,* it went for 400 French francs (about $98 at the time). Since his death, six of his paintings have sold for more than $50 million (£32 million) each!

EAR FOR YOU

Van Gogh suffered from severe depression. Just before Christmas, in 1888, he sliced off part of his left ear while arguing with Paul Gauguin, another famous painter. Van Gogh then gave the chunk of ear to a lady he liked!

A good deal
The *Portrait of Dr. Gachet* was first sold in 1897 for 300 French francs (around $64 at the time). It would change hands several times before being sold in 1990 for a staggering $128 million (£82.5 million).

NICKED!

More than 20 of Van Gogh's paintings have been stolen from galleries and museums. In 1975, *Breton Women* was taken and recovered twice in the space of four months from the Milan Municipal Museum in Italy.

WANT MORE?

In 1888, he completed one painting in a single hour. Go, Van Gogh!

EUROVISION

In the 1950s, a European TV boss liked the idea of a friendly singing competition between nations. Just seven countries took part in the first contest in 1956, won by Switzerland. It's been held every year since. The 2013 edition held in Malmö, Sweden, welcomed singers and bands from 39 European countries in a massive live event watched by around 125 million viewers Europe-wide.

Famous names

Some well-known acts have taken part in Eurovision including Cliff Richard, Katrina and the Waves, and Celine Dion. In 1974, ABBA triumphed for Sweden with their song *Waterloo*, which helped to launch their worldwide pop career.

YOU SHOULD SEE MY REAL FACE!

ROCK ON

Most songs that do well at Eurovision are pop or dance tracks. But in 2006, Finnish heavy rockers Lordi won with *Hard Rock Hallelujah*. With fireworks and scary masks, the act was Finland's first-ever victory.

Scoring points

Each country awards points from 1 to 12 to their favorite 12 entries. Many nations are guilty of block voting—awarding high points to their neighbors. Greece and Cyprus, for example, regularly exchange high marks, as do the UK and Ireland and the former eastern bloc nations Belarus, Ukraine, and Poland.

SMILE DEAR, WE'RE ON TV.

Golden oldies

Age is no obstacle to entering Eurovision. In 2012, the Buranovo Grannies of Russia came second, beating younger acts such as Irish pop duo Jedward!

To celebrate their win, Lordi held a free concert in Helsinki, Finland. 90,000 people showed up!

OH NO, WE'VE BEEN FOILED AGAIN...

Jedward

Winners and losers

Loreen won Sweden's fifth Eurovision in 2012, one of 27 nations to have succeeded. The UK has finished second the most often—a whopping 15 times. Unlucky Malta has finished second twice and third twice. When it comes to losing, Norway are champs, finishing last ten times.

Loreen

MOST SUCCESSFUL

Ireland: 7 wins
France: 5 wins
Luxembourg: 5 wins
Sweden: 5 wins
UK: 5 wins
Netherlands: 4 wins

WANT MORE?

Since 1975, 16 entries have received zero points in the competition. Oh dear.

EUREKA!

ARCHIMEDES

Greece (287–212 BC)

One of the first scientists to use math to explain physical objects and movement. Explained why things float, how levers work, and invented a water pump.

- His shout of "Eureka" on discovering a scientific principle is the motto of California.
- Said to have designed a death ray—it focused the Sun's rays to fry enemy soldiers!

ISAAC NEWTON

England (1642–1727)

Discovered the principles of gravity, produced the three laws of motion that explain how objects move, and built the first reflecting telescope.

- Disguised himself to work undercover on the streets of London, catching fake money-makers.
- Fascinated by alchemy (turning other metals into gold).

LOUIS PASTEUR

France (1822–1885)

Proved that most infectious diseases were caused by microorganisms. Developed ways to stop food from spoiling. Created vaccines against deadly diseases.

- Best subject at school was drawing.
- Investigating rabies, risked his life by taking samples of saliva from the mouths of raging dogs.

EGGHEADS OF EUROPE

Europe has been home to some seriously big brains over the centuries. Many of these scientists have transformed how we see the world. Here, we meet six top scientists, discover what made them famous, and reveal a quirkier side to their lives…

NIKOLA TESLA

Serbia (1856–1943)

Pioneered alternating current (AC) electricity, the type used in most homes today. Transmitted electricity wirelessly, and invented the first radio-controlled model.

- Lived last ten years of his life in a New York hotel, where he fed pigeons.
- Hated shaking hands or touching hair.
- Only stayed in hotel rooms with numbers divisible by three.

MARIE CURIE

Poland (1867–1934)

Investigated radioactivity and discovered, with her husband Pierre, the chemical elements radium and polonium. A pioneer in using X-rays and radiation in medicine.

- First woman to win a Nobel Prize.
- Her notebooks are still too radioactive to handle safely.
- Drove ambulances in World War I.

ALBERT EINSTEIN

Germany (1879–1955)

Huge-brained physicist. His theories changed how people look at space, energy, and matter. He explained how light works and how energy and mass (the amount of something) are related.

- After he died, his brain was removed from his body and pickled in a jar.
- Hated wearing socks and rarely did.

WANT MORE?

More about the world's best scientists ☆ www.famousscientists.org

FUN IN FINLAND

With around 200,000 lakes, Finland is a country of great beauty. Many Finns own a lakeside holiday home, allowing them to enjoy the countryside. But it's not all peace and quiet, as wannabee world champions give it their all—rocking out to seriously loud soundtracks, plowing through water carrying their wives, or tossing their mobile phones as far as they can!

WISH YOU HADN'T EATEN THOSE BEANS!

To have and to hold

The World Wife Carrying Championships have been held in Sonkajärvi since 1992. Racers carry a lady on their backs around a 832 ft-long course (253.5 m). It has two barriers to clamber over and a large water jump to wade through. Crashes and falls occur so the wives wear helmets. Couples are timed and the fastest wins!

Fast and furious

By day, Taisto Miettinen is an ever-so-serious Finnish lawyer, but after work he trains to stay fit, fast, and strong, and with great results. Taisto won four World Wife Carrying Championships in a row between 2009 and 2012.

WIVES RULE!

1. The wife you carry can be yours or someone else's.
2. Wives must weigh at least 108 lb (49 kg).
3. If too light, the wife must wear a backpack loaded with weights.
4. The wife must be at least 17 years of age.

2012 WINNING TIME: 1 minute, 1.22 seconds

CHUGGA-CHUGGA-KERRRRUNNNGG!

Once a year, the Finnish town of Oulu really rocks to the Air Guitar World Championships. Contestants from all over the world mime playing a guitar in front of a crowd of thousands. Judges mark their performance on style, accuracy, and timing with the music. Champions have come from New Zealand, Japan, and the United States.

WHADDAYA MEAN, YOU DON'T LIKE MY SUIT?!

Brrring, brrring fling
Bet you've wanted to chuck your clunky cell phone at some point or another? Well, at Savonlinna, you can, and you might even become a world champion. There's a junior competition for phone throwers under 12, too.

At the weigh-in
Any cell phone weighing at least 8 oz (220 g) is suitable for the competition—but not your parents' latest device, okay? All the broken parts are scooped up afterwards and recycled.

In 2012, Ere Karjalainen from Finland threw his phone 333 ft (101.46 m), a new world record.

= 66 ft (20m)

WANT MORE?

Germany's Aline Westphal became the first female air guitar world champion in 2011.

THE BONE SCULPTOR

Just outside the small Czech town of Kutná Hora, 50 mi (80 km) east of the capital, Prague, lies Sedlec. A monastery was built in Sedlec 900 years ago, and today it is home to the Cemetery Church of All Saints. Nothing remarkable you might think—until you step inside…

Sedlec Ossuary's masterpiece is this incredible chandelier. It's made out of at least one of each of the 206 different bones that make up the human body.

Dishing the dirt

It all started when the head of the monastery, Abbot Jindřich, visited the Middle East in 1278. He returned with soil from the supposed burial site of Jesus Christ and sprinkled it over the cemetery. As word spread, more and more people wanted their loved ones to be buried in the holy soil of Sedlec.

Sedlec Ossuary contains the bones of more than 40,000 skeletons.

THESE BONE-ATIONS ARE VERY NICE . . .

BUT I HAVEN'T GOT ANY BODY TO SPEND THEM ON!

A grave matter

The number of bodies buried at Sedlec soared during the Black Death (see page 86). Soon, there were too many for the cemetery, so a chapel was built for the surplus skeletons. Old graves were also dug up and the bones taken inside. Such stores are called ossuaries.

HERE LYES BURIED
THE BODY OF

SKELETON ARTIST

The bones kept piling up until 1870 when the local Schwarzenberg family bought the chapel. They employed František Rint, a carpenter and woodcarver, to organize all the bones in the chapel. It's fair to say that Rint outdid himself!

Rint arranged the bones to form patterns on the walls and sculptures around the chapel. He hung garlands of leg bones and skulls from the ceiling.

I'VE NEVER HAD A HEAD FOR HEIGHTS!

Coat of bones
František Rint was no fool. He sucked up to his employers big time with this elaborate bony interpretation of the Schwarzenberg family coat of arms.

Bones not alone
One of Europe's biggest ossuaries is in Brno, also in the Czech Republic. It holds around 50,000 skeletons and was only rediscovered in 2001 during building work. Imagine the surprise!

WANT MORE?

See Brno ossuary ☆ www.atlasobscura.com/places/ brno-ossuary

OI! WATCH WHERE YOU'RE GOING.

CANAL HOG!

During the 17th century, there were 10,000 gondolas on Venice's canals.

SO YOU WANT TO BE A GONDOLIER?

The Italian city of Venice is made up of more than 100 islands criss-crossed by a network of 177 canals and more than 400 bridges. Imagine a life as a gondolier, working in the open air, meeting people and seeing the sites as you transport tourists through the scenic canals? Bet it would be a piece of cake to get into? Think it would take next-to-no training? WRONG!

TOP GEAR: GONDOLA

LENGTH: 35.8 ft (10.9 m)
WIDTH: 4.7 ft (1.42 m)
WEIGHT (EMPTY): 1543 lb (700 kg)
ENGINE: 1 oar power
TOP SPEED: about 2.5 mph (4 km/h)
0-60: Are you kidding?
NUMBER OF PARTS: 280
MATERIAL: Eight types of wood: lime, larch, oak, fir, cherry, walnut, elm, and mahogany.

Jobs for the boys... until now
For more than 900 years, gondoliering was only for men. Women had tried and failed the exam until 24-year-old Giorgia Boscolo became the first gondoliera in 2010.

Keep it in the family
Today, there are only 425 gondolas. All are piloted by licensed members of the 1000-year-old Gondolier's Guild. Only a few new licenses are awarded each year, mostly to other family members.

Heavy metal
Il Ferro, "the steel," is a large ornament on the front of a gondola which balances the weight of the back of the boat. The six metal blades symbolize the six historical districts of Venice.

Gone gondoliering
You're looking at serious training time to become a gondolier—more than 400 hours! Then, there's a tough exam that'll test your strength, boat handling, and navigation skills. Gondoliers must know every city site and route. Many fail the test.

Regular gondolas in Venice are painted black, but at festival time blinged-up larger versions take to the canals.

OAR AND PEACE
Modern gondolas are open to the weather. They weigh more than a ton when full of passengers, and are propelled by a single oar. The oar acts as a motor and brakes. It also steers the gondola down crowded canals and during super-tight turns.

WANT MORE?

Early gondola (above) had closed cabins for secret meetings, romance, and kidnappings!

A Spartan army charges into battle.

A SPARTAN LIFE

Growing up as a boy in the ancient Greek city-state of Sparta 2,500 years ago was no picnic. Many Greek states devoted themselves to learning and the arts. Sparta was different. From the 6th century BC onwards, it was warlike and kept a strong army at the ready all the time. So if you think your routine of homework and chores is tough, check out life as a Spartan schoolboy.

Soldier school
As soon as Spartan boys reached seven, they left their families and went to live in army barracks. They slept on the floor and had just one cloak per year to wear. To toughen them up, the boys were underfed, beaten regularly and made to walk barefoot.

THE 300

The Spartan army's most famous battle was actually a defeat in 480 BC. Led by King Leonidas, just 300 Spartans and some 1,100 other Greek soldiers defended Thermopylae against Emperor Xerxes' vast Persian army of more than 100,000. Leonidas' brave lot held out for three days.

Spartan soldiers

Deadly cheese

Boys trained in the arts of fighting and survival. There were no math exams to sweat over, but there was a brutal cheese-stealing contest every year. Competitors tried to snatch cheese from an altar while their classmates flogged them with leather whips. A "fail" in this test often meant boys died from their wounds.

Seven to sixty

All this hard living and training turned boys into super strong warriors. At age 20, they became soldiers of the Spartan army until retiring at 60—if they lived that long! No worries if they didn't, as there were always new kids on the block waiting to replace them.

metal helmet topped with horse hair

large spear

dagger-shaped sword

round shield made of bronze or wood

A Spartan warrior ready for combat

Sparta was no place for weaklings. Tiny or feeble baby boys were often left to die on Mount Taygetos.

WANT MORE?

Black broth (pork cooked in pig's blood) was a typical Spartan soldier's dinner. Yuck!

TOY STORY

What toy is there more than 62 of for every man, woman, and child on the planet? If you answered LEGO® bricks, you'd be right! They were the invention of Ole Kirk Christiansen, a carpenter from Billund in Denmark, and his son Godtfred. Christiansen started out making dull wooden ladders and ironing boards. When sales fell during the 1930s, he had to think of something more fun for people to buy.

> PLASTIC BRICKS, OLE? YOU'RE QUACKERS!

The world's tallest LEGO tower of 2011 was built in Paris, France.

Name of the game
Ole Christiansen made a toy wooden duck for his sons and, seeing how much they liked it, he began producing wooden toys to sell to others. In 1934, he named his business after the Danish words for "play well"— Leg Godt—shortened to LEGO. In a handy coincidence, it turned out that LEGO means "I put together" in Latin.

Father and son of LEGO
Godtfred Christiansen was only four when he and his brother Karl burned down their father's house and workshop while playing with wood shavings. Godtfred owed his father big time! He found a way to repay him in the early 1950s. Together with his dad they dreamt up the idea of toys made of interlocking plastic bricks.

COULD SOMEONE PLEASE GET THIS CAT OFF MY BACK?!

There are 915 million different ways you can combine six eight-studded LEGO bricks.

PARK LIFE

In 1968, Godtfred opened the first LEGOLAND theme park next to the company's factories in Billund. More than 50 million bricks were used to build its exhibits, which are seen by 1.6 million people every year. Five more parks have since opened—In England, Germany, and Malaysia, and two in the USA.

Grown-up LEGO

Adult Fans of LEGO (AFOL) exist all over the world. Some are record breakers. The world record for the tallest LEGO tower has changed hands more than 30 times since 1988. In 2012, a 106.6 ft-high tower (32.5 m) made of 500,000 bricks went up in the Czech city of Prague to become the tallest so far.

Big brick numbers

x5

All the LEGO bricks sold in a year, laid end to end, would circle Earth over five times.

19 billion

19 billion LEGO bricks and other parts are produced every year at the factories in Billund—that's 36,000 pieces every minute.

40 billion

40,000,000,000 LEGO bricks would be needed, stacked on top of each other, to reach the Moon from Earth. Far out!

WANT MORE?

See other LEGO record breakers ✱ www.recordholders.org/en/list/lego.html

SARAJEVO SUN

THE SHOTS THAT SHOOK THE WORLD

In 1914, there was great unrest in Europe. Countries had built up their armed forces as they jostled for power. Smaller regions wanted freedom from larger countries or empires. The whole continent was a time bomb waiting to explode.

HATS OFF TO SARAJEVO.

THE ARCHDUKE AND HIS WIFE, SOPHIE, ARRIVE AT SARAJEVO STATION.

Amateur assassin

A secret group called Black Hand recruited student Gavrilo Princip. His job was to kill Austro-Hungarian heir to the throne, Archduke Franz Ferdinand, during a visit to Sarajevo in Serbia in 1914.

Black Hand

BUMBLING KILLERS!

Gavrilo Princip was not the only assassin. There were another six members of the Black Hand. Each had grenades or bombs, a gun, and a cyanide pill to commit suicide with after the attack.

- The first assassin lost his nerve and let the Archduke's car go past.
- The second lobbed his grenade but it bounced off the car and rolled under a vehicle behind, injuring those inside.
- The Archduke's car sped off and the other assassins, including Princip, gave up and trudged off.

ARE WE NEARLY THERE?

The Black Hand movement wanted freedom from the Austro-Hungarian empire.

MAYHEM ON FRANZ JOSEPH STREET AS PRINCIP SHOOTS...

WRONG WAY

Archduke Ferdinand was outraged at the bungled attack, but later went to visit those who had been injured. A general decided the car should take a different route, but no one told the driver! As he turned into Franz Joseph Street, he was ordered to reverse.

BANG, BANG

Princip was standing outside a shop on Franz Joseph Street. He was surprised to see the Archduke's car right in front of him. As the driver tried to reverse, the car's engine stalled. Princip fired two shots from his gun, killing the Archduke and his wife.

Gavrilo's fate

Princip turned his gun on himself, but was wrestled to the ground. Although charged with double murder, he was too young for the death penalty. He was sent to prison instead, where he died of tuberculosis in 1918.

WORLD AT WAR

Austro-Hungary was outraged and declared war on Serbia on July 28, 1914. The major nations of Europe took sides. Germany and the Ottoman Empire supported Austro-Hungary. Russia, Britain, and France all entered the war on the side of Serbia. World War I (1914–1918) became the largest and most destructive war the world had ever seen.

WANT MORE?

Read all about it ☆ www.firstworldwar.com/source/harrachmemoir.htm

All you can eat

Lotito started munching serious metal objects—from bicycles to beds—in his teens. He swallowed small pieces washed down with mineral oil and lots of water. Doctors found he had a stomach lining twice as thick as normal.

IN AND OUT

Humans need a little iron in their diet, but one man took it to extremes. Born in Grenoble, France, Michel Lotito (1950–2007) had a strange urge to eat metal, glass, and rubber things. It began when his parents caught him gnawing their old television set. His nickname was Monsieur Mangetout (Mr. Eats All).

By 1997, Monsieur Mangetout had chomped more than 9 tons (8 tonnes) of metal!

It was the first time a coffin ended up inside a man instead of the man ending up inside a coffin!

On Monsieur Mangetout's

MENU

18 bicycles

15 supermarket trolleys

7 TV sets

6 chandeliers

2 beds

1 pair of skis

1 coffin

In-flight dining
Like your food plain?
Well, Lotito liked planes
as food! His greatest
extreme eating act took
two years (1979–1980).
He ate an entire Cessna
150 light aircraft—
propeller, wings, and all.

MMM, A TASTY,
LIGHT SNACK.

WINDY CITY

Another unique Frenchman
was Joseph Pujol (1857–1945).
He could suck in and blow out
air through his bottom at will.
Paris became the windy city
during the 1890s when Pujol
starred at the famous Moulin
Rouge Theatre.

For a time, Pujol
was the highest-paid
entertainer in France,
earning around the
wages of 250 school
teachers
at once.

LE PÉTOMANE

Tous les soirs

AU MOULIN ROUGE

Candles in the wind
Pujol used his unusual skill to
imitate musical instruments
and farm animals. He could
play tunes, including the
French national anthem, and
could blow out candles from
a distance. King Leopold II of
Belgium and Prince Edward
of Wales were amongst his
many fans.

WANT
MORE?

Watch Michel munch metal ☆ www.youtube.com/watch?v=h6Pl2-lx12A

THE EMPIRE STRIKES BACK

Europe has had more than its fair share of grand empires. But from the 15th century onwards, a new power really put Europe to the test. The Ottoman, or Turkish, Empire captured Constantinople in 1453. They renamed it Istanbul and made it the center of an empire that grew fast and furious. Ruthlessness and brutality were two of many reasons for the Empire's success.

Sultan Mehmed II's army surrounds Constantinople, 1453.

THOSE EUROPEANS DON'T STAND A CHANCE AGAINST US.

IT'LL SOON BE GONE-STANTINOPLE!

One king to rule all

The Ottoman Empire concentrated power in one ruler, the Sultan, so decisions could be made fast. On coming to power, some sultans had their brothers murdered so they couldn't plot and overthrow them.

CAN'T THINK WHY I'VE GOT A HEADACHE!

Sultan Suleiman I (1494–1566)

Fighting forces

Ottoman armies were fierce and brave in battle. Under skilled generals, such as Sultans Mehmed II and Suleiman I, they conquered much of Eastern Europe. Their elite troops, called Janissaries, were well-drilled, well-paid, and lived together as a tight-knit unit.

A Janissary

YOU'RE FIRED!

Ottoman armies combined brutal hand-to-hand fighting methods with more modern guns and cannons. The Great Turkish Bombard was a huge cannon, which could fire a giant cannonball as far as 2 miles (3 km). This powerful weapon helped destroy the walls of Constantinople.

Topkapi Palace

Making an example
From the moment you reached the Sultan's home in Istanbul, you knew he meant business. Displayed outside the Imperial Gate of Topkapi Palace were the heads of freshly executed criminals. Inside the palace, the stuffed heads of nobles who'd angered the Sultan were placed on marble pillars, called example stones.

The tughra was the official signature or seal of a sultan.

Soft in the head
The heads of executed major nobles were cut off and stuffed with soft cotton. Those of less important nobles were stuffed with straw.

I'M FEELNG A BIT FUZZY-HEADED!

Tughra used as sultan's signature on official documents

It wasn't all war, war, war
Some sultans proved skilled at non-military matters, creating schools, and boosting trade. Suleiman I, for example, revamped Istanbul by building 26 libraries, 17 hospitals, and 132 mosques. He encouraged many arts including calligraphy.

WANT MORE?

During Sultan Selim I's eight-year rule, 30,000 people were executed.

Europeans are crazy about soccer. In fact it's the continent's favorite sport. Europe is home to many of the world's greatest soccer teams, or "clubs," from Bayern Munich, Germany, to Manchester United, UK. It's packed with teams, big and small, who are fiercely competitive. When they play each other, the rivalry is called a "derby." Watch the sparks fly!

SUPER STADIA

For a derby game, or "match," to really buzz you need a great stadium packed with fans. The biggest team stadium in Europe is Barcelona's Camp Nou ground in Spain, which holds more than 98,000 spectators.

SOCCER CRAZEEEE!

German soccer teams, such as Schalke and Borussia Dortmund, pack out their games. The country's top 36 teams sold 18.8 million tickets in the 2011/2012 season.

Turkish delight

Turkey is home to a fearsome derby between Fenerbahçe and Galatasaray. Fenerbahçe have won more games, but Galatasaray supporters still brag about their biggest-ever win of 7–0 in 1911. This is even more impressive given that Galatasaray only had seven players.

Fenerbahçe fans fly the flag outside their home stadium in Istanbul.

COME ON, WHERE ARE YOU?

The biggest thrashing ever in an El Clásico derby saw Real Madrid beat Barcelona 11-1 in 1943.

Lionel Messi scored 73 goals in the 2011/2012 season—a European record.

OVER HERE, BEHIND THE GOAL.

GO AND PLAY ON THE WING!

Cristiano Ronaldo

Lionel Messi

Mascot madness

Many European soccer teams have a cuddly mascot to greet younger fans. Occasionally, the mascots go derby day crazy and push or even fight their opponent.

REIGN IN SPAIN

The big El Clásico derby in Spain is between the country's two most successful teams: Real Madrid and Barcelona. These teams are packed with the greatest players around. Real have Cristiano Ronaldo—the world's highest-paid soccer player at about $42 million (£27.5 million) per year. Barcelona have Lionel Messi—the world's best player.

WANT MORE?

EXTINCT IN EUROPE

OH DEAR, THIS IS AUK-WARD. PLEASE DON'T SHOOT!

Europe may have less extreme wildlife than other continents, but it's still home to monkeys (barbary macaques in Gibraltar), wild boar, gray wolves, and more than 30 species of bat. Sadly, some of its more exotic creatures have died out during past centuries. These include the great auk, a hefty seabird once found on islands throughout northernmost Europe.

Sitting ducks

Great auks were hunted for thousands of years. Originally, they were snared for their meat and eggs. But from the 15th to 17th centuries their feathers became highly prized for stuffing pillows. Quick underwater, the birds were clumsy on land and easy to catch.

FOR SALE
$450

FOR SALE
$450

In the 19th century, you could buy a small house in Europe for the price of a 5-inch-long great auk's egg (12 cm)— $450 (£300).

The more great auk numbers plummeted, the more they were hunted. Europe's museums were booming and all wanted auks (dead or alive) for their displays. The last known pair of birds were killed by Icelandic fishermen in 1844.

Auks' end
The last great auk in Britain was killed in 1840 by three sailors who feared it was a witch. Doh!

Recently departed
Other large European animals have also become extinct since the great auk. These include the Caspian tiger, which inhabited Georgia, Turkey, and Russia until the mid-20th century. The last tarpan died in Poland in 1879. The pied raven of the Faroe Islands died out in 1948. And the last Pyrenean ibex died in 2000.

Tarpan

Pyrenean ibex

I FEEL A HEADACHE COMING ON...

EXOTIC EXTINCTIONS
European lions once roamed Greece and the Balkans. Parts of Europe were also home to European cheetahs, cave hyenas, and Eurasian aurochs (giant wild cattle). There were also Irish elks with 13-foot-wide (4 m) antlers.

WHO ARE YOU CALLING SHORTY?

Irish elk

Tiny tusks
Cyprus was once home to its own species of pygmy hippos and dwarf elephants. These stunted mammals stood no taller than 35 in (90 cm). Ah, cute!

Pygmy hippo

Cave hyena skull

WANT MORE?

Declared extinct in 1962, Bavarian pine voles were rediscovered in Austria in 2000.

PETER'S PLACE

WHERE'S ALL THE SEA GONE?

In 2012, St. Petersburg's population passed five million. Russia's second-largest city is also its most westernized, and for that one can thank (or blame) their former ruler, Tsar Peter I (1672–1725), or Peter the Great. Fascinated by ships as a child, Peter knew his country needed sea ports in the Baltic to trade with other nations. He went to war with Sweden to capture new territory.

CAN'T WAIT TO GET MY KING'S CLOTHES BACK ON.

On tour
In 1697, Peter left Russia and toured Europe, learning about how other countries were run. He worked as an ordinary laborer in the Dutch shipyards. Peter returned a big fan of western ways. He was determined to modernize Russia.

Monument of Peter the Great in Moscow, Russia

Peter dressed as a carpenter on his European tour.

On tour Peter disguised himself as a ship's carpenter called Peter Mikhailov. He fooled no one. At 6.7 ft (2.04 m), he was one of Europe's tallest men and towered over almost everyone he met.

WAR AND PETE

St. Petersburg was founded in 1703 when Peter's armies grabbed the Neva River delta, an area of swampy land and islands in the Gulf of Finland. There, they built the Peter and Paul Fortress (above). The first building erected was a three-roomed wooden cabin for Peter. It was built in just three days and still stands today.

Tsar quality

Peter moved his capital from Moscow to his new city in St. Petersburg in 1712. It was one of many sweeping changes he introduced. The Tsar formed Russia's navy and built the country's first modern hospitals. He encouraged mining, industry, and trade. He discouraged forced marriage and old ways of living.

One of the prisoners in the Peter and Paul Fortress was Peter's own son, Alexei. He was tortured and died there in 1718.

BUT I CAN AFFORD TO PAY FOR IT!

Off with their beards

Under Peter, old fashions and beards were out. He personally and brutally cut off nobles' beards and slashed their traditional clothes. Anyone desperate to keep their beard had to pay a massive tax for the privilege.

WANT MORE?

Prankster Peter built trick fountains at his palace, Peterhof, to soak nobles to the skin.

Kings and queens once ruled most of Europe, but how many of those countries have reigning royalty today? One? Two? The answer is ten. Can you name them all?* Now, if you think kings and queens are dusty old figures you only read about in history books, you may be in for a surprise as you check out these fun-loving royals.

WE ARE MOST AMUSED.

KINGS AND QUEENS OF EUROPE

OUT WITH THE OLD THRONE!

King Willem-Alexander

Meet brand new Dutch monarch Willem-Alexander. He took charge in 2013 after his mother, Queen Beatrix stepped down. The new king's an all-action kind of guy, having run the New York marathon, competed in an ice skating marathon, and piloted a jet aircraft.

The king takes part in a toilet-throwing competition on Queen's Day in the Netherlands

King Willem-Alexander

Queen Margrethe II

Margrethe II is the first queen of Denmark to rule by herself. This talented queen's paintings have appeared in many major European exhibitions and she illustrated the Danish edition of *The Lord of the Rings*. She's also a fashion designer whose costumes have appeared in ballets and in movies.

Queen Margrethe II

*Ten Thrones: Belgium, Britain, Denmark, the Netherlands, Norway, Spain, Sweden, Liechtenstein, Monaco, and Luxembourg.

Queen Elizabeth II
The 40th British monarch since William the Conqueror in 1066, Queen Elizabeth II has reigned for more than 60 years. But far from being locked in the past, the Queen launched her own website in 1997 and sent her first email in 1976—long before you did!

QUEEN ELIZABETH II BY NUMBERS

Ships launched:
21

Letters received:
3.5 million

THE QUEEN
Buckingham Palace
London

Telegrams to people celebrating 100th birthdays:
175,000

Official overseas visits made:
more than 250

Christmas puddings given to staff:
90,000

THE KING'S HERE... GULP!

King Juan Carlos
Fond of taking anonymous cross-country motorbike rides, the king of Spain speaks five languages and has hunted bears (which upsets some of his subjects). Juan Carlos also competed at the 1972 Olympic games, sailing yachts.

Monaco's reigning monarch, Prince Albert II, competed at five Winter Olympics in the bobsleigh.

WANT MORE?

Check out Europe's royalty ☆ www.royaltymonarchy.com/royfacts/current.html

VIVA PASTA

If you believe the cliché of Italians loving their lasagna and linguine and slurping their spaghetti… then you'd be right! No one makes or eats more pasta than the average Italian—more than 57 lb (26 kg) of the stuff each year. That's a good 100–150 meals worth a year and double that of any other country.

In the distant pasta

No one knows who actually invented pasta. But we know it was being made in China and in Arabia hundreds of years ago. It was even eaten by the Etruscans, who lived in the area that is now Italy more than 2,400 years ago!

Footing the bill

Pasta was originally made by hand or, in Italy, by feet. The tough dough was kneaded by workers treading on it for up to a day before it was rolled out. Thankfully, Cesare Spadaccini invented a machine to replace the footwork in the 19th century.

Simply does it

There are more than 600 types and shapes of pasta. Some types are made fresh with egg. Others consist of flour, water, and salt, which is then dried for up to 50 hours.

PASTA TRANSLATION

PASTA NAME		MEANING
Linguine		Little tongues
Fettuccine		Ribbons
Vermicelli		Little worms
Farfalle		Butterflies
Tortellini		Little pies

I'M A SUCKER FOR SPAGHETTI!

Italian Ernesto Cesario holds the world record for eating a full bowl of pasta in just 90 seconds. Mamma mia!

I WISH PIZZAS GREW ON TREES, TOO!

Pasta mix-up

Despite being a simple dish, some people outside Italy found pasta a bit mysterious. Thousands of Brits were tricked by an April Fool's Day hoax in 1957. A TV documentary showed a Swiss family harvesting spaghetti from trees!

3.6 million tons

WANT MORE?

Italy makes 3.6 million tons (3.3 million tonnes) of pasta every year.

UNFINISHED BUSINESS

Antoni Gaudí (1852–1926) graduated from Barcelona's School of Architecture, Spain, in 1878. Its director said aloud, "Gentlemen, we are here today in the presence of either a genius or a madman." For much of Gaudí's life, people remained undecided.

Gaudí planned the Sagrada Familia to have 18 towering spires, the tallest rising 558 ft (170 m). Eight were in place by 2010.

YOU'VE GOT TO THINK BIG...

Antoni Gaudí

When complete, the church will hold up to 9,000 people!

Started small, finished BIG

Gaudí's first job as an architect was nothing more grand than a set of lamp posts for squares in Barcelona. But he soon got bigger commissions, and in 1883 began work on his masterpiece, a giant new church in Barcelona—the Sagrada Familia.

Sagrada Familia

Slow progress

Gaudí was a perfectionist and took his time. He preferred making models to producing building plans and wasn't worried by delays. When he was killed by a tram in 1926, the Sagrada Familia was less than a quarter completed. Work continues to this day, with the hope that it will be completed in 2026.

OH, MY HEAD!

To see how a donkey statue would look high up on part of the church, Gaudí had a real live one lifted up by cranes working on the church.

Antoni's antics

Gaudí was a vegetarian, never married, was famous for his short temper, and insisted on wearing shabby suits. He also preferred second-hand shoes, so he got his brother Francesc to wear in new pairs for him first.

PARK LIFE

Barcelona's Park Güell was built between 1900 and 1916. Gaudí designed it as a city park, full of fairytale buildings and mosaic tiles.

Dragon at Park Güell

After he died, Gaudí was buried in the crypt of his unfinished church.

WANT MORE?

The Sagrada Familia church is almost the size of a soccer field.

Stretching across eight countries, from Slovenia to France, the Alps mountain range is packed full of peaks. More than 80 of these reach 13,123 ft (4,000 m) or above. Today, thousands of climbers attempt to scale them for the challenge. But less than 200 years ago most peaks had yet to be climbed.

Mont Blanc

The tallest of the Alps, Mont Blanc, was one of the first to be conquered in 1786. The two-man team of Jacques Balmat and Michel-Gabriel Paccard didn't use ropes or ice axes. Their only climbing equipment was an alpenstock—a long wooden pole with an iron spike on one end.

Memorial plaque to Balmat and Paccard

TO THE SUMMIT

I'M FEELING A LITTLE PEAKY...

Drawing on experience

Edward Whymper was a young illustrator who traveled to the Alps in 1860 to draw scenes of the mountains. He quickly fell under their spell and learned how to climb from local guides. In 1864, he was part of the first group to climb Barre des Écrins in the Alps. He was also the first to climb five other Alpine peaks in 1864 and 1865.

Edward Whymper

The murderous Matterhorn

Whymper's biggest mountaineering test was the mighty Matterhorn. He made eight failed attempts to climb it before he succeeded in 1865. Hours after the success came tragedy when four of his seven-man party fell to their deaths on the way down.

HELP, I'M STUCK!

The towering peak of the Matterhorn

WATCH OUT!

I SHOULDN'T HAVE ROPED YOU INTO THIS.

More than 500 people have perished climbing the Matterhorn since Whymper's ascent.

Modern-day climbers wear helmets and fleeces.

A GOLDEN AGE

The mid-19th century is known as the golden age of Alpinism. It's when most of the major peaks were climbed (the last being Meije in 1877). Many of the climbers wore jackets and ties but no protective helmets. Nor did they have GPS, fleeces, or other hi-tech climbing gear.

19th-century climbers wearing everyday clothing.

WANT MORE?

In 2007, Slovenian Miha Valič climbed 82 Alpine peaks in just 102 days.

THINKING MAN

I THINK... I NEED A SHAVE!

Leonardo da Vinci

You've probably got friends who are great at more than one thing. Annoying, aren't they? Well imagine being Leonardo da Vinci's pal! The Renaissance (14th–17th centuries) was when Europe woke up and really started thinking about things. Leonardo da Vinci (1452–1519) was the ultimate Renaissance man. He was a thinker, painter, engineer, inventor, and scientist. Oh, and he also played a mean lyre (stringed instrument).

A lyre

Paint job
Leo often switched from one artwork to another and left many unfinished and now lost. Some of his works that have survived include the mysterious *Mona Lisa* and the enormous 29 ft-long (8.8 m) mural of *The Last Supper*.

Mona Lisa

The Last Supper

LEONARDO DA VINCI **MONA LISA**

4 Ft MAGYAR POSTA

THAT MINESTRONE WAS SOUPER.

I CAN'T BELIEVE HE ATE ALL YOUR CHIPS!

Body of work

Leo's interest in anatomy saw him dissect human corpses to learn the secrets inside. He filled notebook upon notebook of detailed sketches. These included his famous Vitruvian Man sketch. It shows how each part of the human body is in proportion.

Vitruvian Man, 1490

Leonardo was a vegetarian and often bought caged birds which he released into the wild.

x6 = your height

3D model of the ornithopter

Measure your foot then multiply by six. The answer should be close to your height. Thanks, Leo!

Amongst da Vinci's sketches and plans were a mechanical flying bat, called an ornithopter, and winged boots for walking on water!

Model of the armored boat designed by Leo

Ahead of his time

Leo drew plans for devices that the world wouldn't see for centuries. His ideas included helicopters and parachutes, the bicycle, solar power, and an armored tank that could carry eight men. Some of his inventions, such as lens grinding machines, were built and became a great success.

WANT MORE?

Da Vinci wrote all his notes backward, possibly to keep them secret!

Superyacht marina in Monaco.

HOT SPOTS

You're an uber-rich celebrity with money to burn. Perhaps you'd kick back and relax on your own private island, like shipping magnate Aristotle Onassis (owner of the Greek island of Skorpios) or Portuguese soccer player Cristiano Ronaldo (who owns Deserta Island near Madeira). Or, you might glide around the most luxurious hot spots seeking out the best and most expensive Europe has to offer.

Luxury travel

In the past, you might take the luxurious Orient Express train from Paris in France to Istanbul in Turkey. But today you're just as likely to jet in to a private airstrip or sail your superyacht into an exclusive members-only marina at Monaco, Capri, Portafino, or Hvar in Croatia.

The best rooms in Hotel President Wilson in Geneva, Switzerland, can cost $65,000 (£42,000) a night. Ouch!

BEST room

BRMMM, BRMMM

If cars are your thing, head to the French-German border. This is where Bugatti build the world's fastest and most expensive supercar—the Veyron 16.4 Super Sport. A souped-up Veyron can reach 268 mph (431 km/h) and could set you back $3.2 million (£2.1 million).

HUNGRY FOR SUCCESS

Millionaires might plump for a Seafood Treasure curry at London's Bombay Brasserie. A bargain at $3,000 (£2,000) per person! Or perhaps a meal at Solo Per Due—an entire restaurant in Varone, Italy, for just two dinner guests. Until it closed in 2011, Spain's El Bulli eaterie lavished guests with 30-course meals which took five hours to eat!

$3,000

100

25

PLEASE DON'T LET ANYONE SEE ME LIKE THIS!

Pampered pooches

Every year fashionistas head for the catwalk shows in Milan, Paris, London, and Madrid. For glittering jewels, Antwerp in Belgium is the place to go. More than 60% of the world's diamonds are traded there. A diamond dog collar could set you back $155,440 (£100,000)!

WHEEL OF FORTUNE

Wealthy gamblers head to Monaco to try their luck at the Monte Carlo Casino. In 1873, ten years after the casino opened, British engineer Joseph Jagger won big time. He was the first player to break the bank.

Stinking rich

In the past, European royals and nobles drenched themselves and their rooms in scent to mask the stench of body odor and poor sanitation. Today, Guerlain is one of France's leading perfume houses. Its special edition Idylle fragrance comes in an 18-carat-gold bottle that you have to break to open, and costs almost $47,000 (£30,000).

DARLING, I'M WORTH IT!

50

WANT MORE?

In 2011, a flat in One Hyde Park in London sold for $207 million (£136 million)!

SPY CITY

If you were a spy in the years after World War II, Berlin was the place to be. The German city was crawling with undercover agents and informers. Berlin marked the border between a Europe divided in two. It was split into those nations in the West, allied to the United States, and those in the East, supported by the Soviet Union. Both sides in the Cold War (1945–1990) tried all sorts of tricks to steal secrets from each other.

ANYONE HERE NOT A SPY?

Split city, two countries
After World War II, Germany was split into two countries, East and West Germany. The border between the two countries ran through the center of Berlin. Both sides in the Cold War confronted each other head-to-head.

TOP SECRET

Tiny cameras were fitted inside ties and suit jackets to snap spies and secrets without anyone knowing.

CAN'T CATCH ME!

Markus Wolf

The man with no face
Top East German spymaster Markus Wolf was so shady, it took the West 25 years to snap a photograph of him. Wolf placed hundreds of spies throughout Berlin, and even inside the West German government. One of his opponents, West German spymaster Hans Joachim Tiedge, turned out to be an East German spy recruited by Wolf!

US soldiers on patrol at a border crossing between East and West Berlin.

Bridge of spies

If you were caught as a spy, death or imprisonment were likely options. Sometimes, though, the two sides would exchange captured enemy agents. Many of these spy swaps occurred on the edge of Berlin at Glienicke Bridge.

In 1985, the largest spy swap saw 27 spies exchanged on Glienicke Bridge.

The spy tunnel is uncovered by East Germans in 1956.

Going underground

A daring mission in the 1950s saw British and American spies dig a top-secret tunnel under East Berlin so that East German phone lines could be tapped and calls listened to. The tunnel was discovered in 1956, but not before around 440,000 phone calls had been recorded.

1,476 ft-long tunnel (450 m) **440,000** phone calls

WANT MORE?

Read about the Cold War ☆ www.ducksters.com/history/cold_war/berlin_wall.php

THE EARTH TURNS I TELL YOU!

SEEING STARS

During the 16th and 17th centuries, Europeans were so self-centered they thought the Sun, the planets, and the entire universe moved around Earth. Today, we know it isn't all about us. But at the time, few dared to question this view, especially as it was supported by the all-powerful Church. It took a ridiculously smart and rebellious scientist to provide the proof. His name? Galileo Galilei (1564–1642).

Making a spectacle of yourself

In 1609, Galileo heard about Dutch spectacle makers who fitted two lenses in a tube to view distant objects. Galileo soon whipped up his own version. It only offered three-times (3x) magnification. But he quickly developed more powerful lenses. Galileo created an 8x telescope which he showed off to the bigwigs of Venice.

Galileo's views of the moon through his telescope.

Looking up

By the winter of 1609, Galileo had built a 20x telescope. This is when things got really interesting. He mapped stars in the night sky and tracked the movement of sunspots. He spotted the rings of Saturn, saw the craters of the Moon, and discovered four moons orbiting Jupiter—Europa, Ganymede, Io, and Callisto.

Book good, book bad

Galileo's observations proved that Earth and other planets moved around the Sun. And that the Sun spun on its own axis—revolutionary! He wrote down what he learned in two books. The first, *The Starry Messenger*, was a bestseller. The second, *Dialogue*, got him into serious trouble.

Galileo's *Dialogue* book stayed on the Church's list of banned books for more than 200 years.

RACE YOU TO THE BOTTOM!

An arresting story

Galileo was put on trial by the Church for his views on the universe in 1633. Found guilty, he was placed under house arrest for the rest of his life.

A towering solution

Galileo loved to prove the old ideas wrong. In his time, most scientists believed heavy objects fell faster than lighter ones. According to legend, Galileo proved otherwise by dropping one light and one much heavier cannonball from the top of the Leaning Tower of Pisa, Italy. Both reached the ground at the same time.

Galileo 1
Aristotle 0

Galileo spacecraft

Some 350 years after Galileo's death, the spacecraft named after him was launched by shuttle. The spacecraft entered Jupiter's atmosphere for a close-up look.

WANT MORE?

More on Galileo ☆ http://galileo.rice.edu/galileo.html

STRANGE GAMES

The Olympic Games has two starting points, more than 2,600 years apart. In 776 BC, the ancient Greeks began holding a festival at Olympia every four years. The games lasted for about 1,000 years until they were abolished by the Romans. In the 1880s, Frenchman Baron Pierre de Coubertin held the first modern Olympics in Athens. Seven out of the first eight Olympics were held in European cities, but the games are now a massive global event.

I LOVE GAMES, I REALLY DO!

Baron Pierre de Coubertin

ROPED IN

A popular event at early Olympics was the tug of war. In 1900, Edgar Aaybe, a journalist, was literally roped in when the Danish team found themselves a man short. The team won and Edgar became an unlikely gold medallist.

Early errors

Early Olympics would not have won gold for organization. At the Paris 1900 games, Margaret Abbot won the women's golf competition but wasn't told. She lived the rest of her life not knowing she was an Olympic champ. At the 1920 games in Antwerp, Belgium, the cycle course ran across railway lines. Some cyclists had to stop at a level crossing for four minutes to let a train go past.

EURO-LYMPICS: THEN AND NOW

Athens 1896 ( )
London 2012 ✏

	Athletes	Women	Nations	Events
Athens 1896	245	0	14	43
London 2012	10,820	4,847	204	302

The 1896 Olympic stadium was made of white marble.

I'M GOING ROUND THE BEND!

Greek games
The ancient Greek Olympics started with just one sports event, a running race called a stade. Over time, events such as wrestling, javelin, and long jump were added.

The reigning tug of war champs remain the City of London Police Force, winners in 1920. One of their team, Robert Spear, was banned for yanking the rope so hard that it pulled an opponent's arm out of its socket. Ouch!

Odd events
The Athens 1896 games featured rope climbing, one-handed weightlifting, and a swimming race only for Greek sailors. The Paris 1900 games had hot-air ballooning, the horse long jump, and the grisly sport of live pigeon shooting. The 1908 London games included the standing long jump (no run-up allowed), and motorboating.

Live pigeon shooting

Standing long jump at the 1908 Olympics

WISH THEY'D HURRY UP AND INVENT DEODORANT!

WANT MORE?

Learn about the early games ☆ **www.olympic.org/ancient-olympic-games**

You're a humble peasant farmer in the 9th or 10th century, peacefully planting crops or tending your few chickens by the coast. Suddenly, something appears on the horizon… trouble with a capital "V:" It's a Viking raid! Before you know it, your village has been robbed, the church plundered, and buildings burned down. Your best friends have been slaughtered or captured as slaves.

BY THE POWER OF ODIN!

Viking raiders on the rampage

Meet your enemy

Vikings were warlike members of Norse peoples who lived in Scandinavia. For almost 300 years, they raided and invaded much of the coastline of northern Europe. They went into battle equipped with large swords or battleaxes, spears, shields, and plenty of attitude.

WHAT YOU LOOKING AT?

MY NAME IS FIERCE!

Lethal weapons

Viking swords were 28–32 in (70–80 cm) long and double-edged. Owners often gave them names such as *Gramr* (Fierce) or *Fotbitr* (Leg-biter).

I SPY A NORSE BIT OF LAND AHEAD!

BERSERKERS!

If you thought regular Viking warriors were bad enough, check out the Berserkers. These bear or wolfskin-clad nuts worked themselves up into a frenzy or ate drugged food before battle. Either way, they ran wild, oblivious to fear or pain. They truly believed they were invincible… and often were.

Gods on their side

The Vikings believed their Norse gods encouraged war. Thor, for example, was always on the warpath. His father, Odin, the main man, looked after Valhalla. This was the Vikings' heaven in the form of a giant feasting hall. Only Viking warriors who died gloriously in battle were allowed entry.

Odin on his eight-legged horse

SURPRISE, SURPRISE

Viking raids were sudden and brutal. These Norse warriors were expert sailors and navigators. Their flat-bottomed longboats, propelled by sails and oars, could travel up rivers or shallow water at speed. Once onshore, Vikings attacked without delay, killing or stealing everything in their path.

Adventurous viking

Viking explorer Leif Eriksson (c. 970–1020) is believed to have reached North America around 1,000 years ago. An 11th-century Viking settlement has been found at L'Anse aux Meadows in Newfoundland, Canada.

Statue of Leif Eriksson

WANT MORE?

Discover more about the Vikings ☆ **www.jorvik-viking-centre.co.uk**

TOPPLED!

Between 1989 and 1991,
Europe lost two countries
(East Germany and
the Soviet Union) and
gained a whole lot more.
The Soviet Union had
been the world's largest
superpower but in 1991, it dissolved
into 15 different nations. Symbols
of the Soviet Union, particularly its
hammer and sickle flag, and many
statues of Soviet leaders,
were toppled or destroyed.

BERLIN

French sector

West

British sector

Soviet sector

East

American sector

Tear down the wall
As the Soviet Union eased its grip
on eastern Europe, East Germany
and West Germany were reunited
as one country. The Berlin Wall,
which had split the city
in two for almost 30 years,
was torn down with relish
by Germans.

HEY!
STOP SITTING
ON ME.

Germans old and
young became
Mauerspechte—wall
woodpeckers. They
chiselled out
chunks of the
Berlin Wall as
souvenirs.

Less is gor
Mikhail Gorbachev was born in 1931.
He became Soviet President in 1985.
Gorbachev introduced reforms
including glasnost which
saw more freedoms for
people. He removed Soviet
troops from eastern
European countries such
as Hungary and
East Germany.

WE'RE FREE!

In September 1991, the three Baltic states of Latvia, Estonia and Lithuania broke away from the Soviet Union. They became independent again after being swallowed up by the Soviets in 1944. Statues of former Soviet leaders such as Josef Stalin and Vladimir Lenin were toppled.

A map of eastern Europe after the Soviet Union broke up in 1991.

—— Border of the Soviet Union before its collapse.

Toppled statue of Vladimir Lenin in Vilnius, Lithuania.

Statue park

More than 20 years later, a theme park in Lithuania has turned back time. It features more than 80 rescued statues of Soviet leaders along with actors playing roles of communist party workers and Soviet guards. More than 200,000 visit each year!

Stalin lying in Vilnius, Lithuania.

HONEST, I'M ARMLESS.

WHO ARE YOU CALLING GORBY?

WANT MORE?

Mikhail Gorbachev won the Nobel Peace Prize in 1990.

THE PRANCING HORSE

Europe is the home of many legendary sports cars from Lamborghini in Italy to Porsche in Germany. Few are more famous than Ferrari. The supersleek vehicles, mostly in racing red, were the brainchild of a speed freak called Enzo Ferrari (1898–1988). He began his adult life as a blacksmith in the Italian Army during World War I.

WISH I'D REMEMBERED MY BOOSTER SEAT.

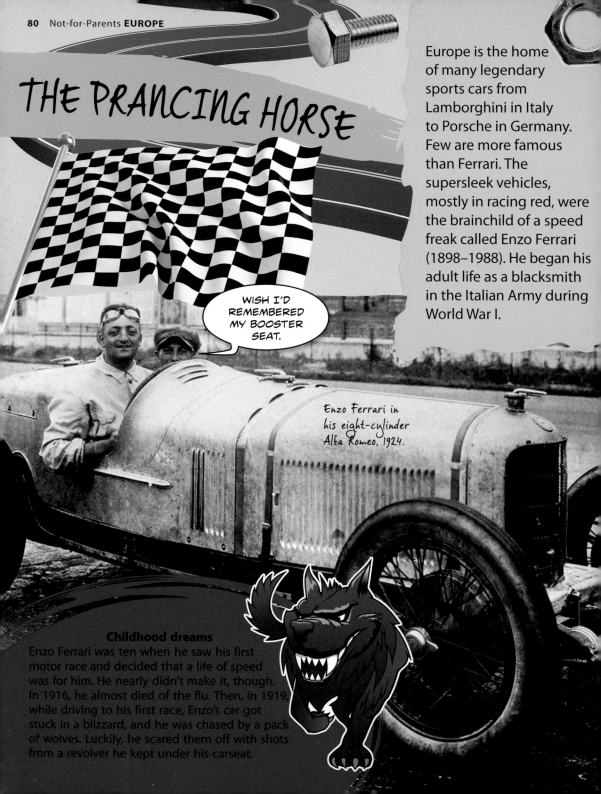

Enzo Ferrari in his eight-cylinder Alfa Romeo, 1924.

Childhood dreams

Enzo Ferrari was ten when he saw his first motor race and decided that a life of speed was for him. He nearly didn't make it, though. In 1916, he almost died of the flu. Then, in 1919, while driving to his first race, Enzo's car got stuck in a blizzard, and he was chased by a pack of wolves. Luckily, he scared them off with shots from a revolver he kept under his carseat.

BADGE OF HONOR

In 1923, Enzo won a race at Ravenna in Italy. It was watched by the mother of Count Francesco Baracca, a World War I fighter pilot. She asked Enzo to use the symbol painted on her son's plane for good luck. Today, all Ferraris come with the famous black prancing horse on a yellow background. Yellow is the color of Ferrari's home city of Modena.

Racing and riding
To begin with, Ferrari's race teams drove Alfa Romeos. But Enzo began to make his own sports cars after World War II. Ferrari also ran his own Formula One team which has since won more than 200 races and 31 world championships.

In 2012, 964 Ferrari cars, the most ever in one place, roared around the Silverstone race circuit in the UK.

GTO TO GO

One of the most exclusive Ferraris of all was the Ferrari 250 GTO. Only 39 of these were made between 1962 and 1964. In 2012, two of these rare vehicles were sold, one for $31.2 million (£20.2 million) and another for $3 million more.

SOLD
$31.2 million

WANT MORE?

In 1985, a sales brochure for a Ferrari 250 GTO car sold for $1,627 (£1,070).

THE EMPEROR OF ELBA

Napoleon Bonaparte (1769–1821) was a mighty general and Emperor of France. He was the most feared man in Europe until, in April 1814, he was forced to sign away his power. The Treaty of Fontainebleau saw him exiled to Elba, a small island in the Mediterranean Sea. France appointed a new ruler, King Louis XVIII, and Europe moved on. Napoleon, nicknamed Boney by British troops, appeared to be yesterday's man… but was he?

WE'LL FOLLOW. BONEY'S BACK!

I WAS THE MOST FAMOUS, POWERFUL MAN IN THE WORLD!

COURSE YOU WERE, DEAR…

Napoleon's first wife was called Rose but he didn't like the name, so called her Josephine instead.

Exiled in Elba
Napoleon tried to improve life on Elba. He surveyed the land, ordered hospitals to be built, and drilled his tiny army of several hundred loyal soldiers who accompanied him from France. His mother and sister joined him in exile but his wife, Marie Louise, refused. What a spoilsport!

Escape from Elba
About 300 days after he arrived, Napoleon ditched Elba. There were spies on the island and ships from other countries keeping watch around the coast. But Napoleon and a handful of his loyal guards managed to escape by grabbing a ship and sailing to the French coast.

KILL ME OR FOLLOW ME!

March to power

Napoleon marched towards Paris, his tiny force swelling into a large army. Many Frenchmen remained big fans. French soldiers were sent to capture him at Grenoble, but instead joined forces with him. As he arrived in Paris, in March 1815, King Louis XVIII fled to Belgium. Boney was back!

WATERLOO

Napoleon again threatened to conquer Europe but his opponents joined forces. British and Prussian armies defeated him at the Battle of Waterloo, in June 1815. It was game over for Boney! He was exiled again, but given no power. This time, he was sent to the isolated island of St. Helena, in the middle of the Atlantic Ocean, for the rest of his life.

St. Helena is 1,180 mi (1,900 km) west of Angola.

OUCH!

Over a third of Napoleon's 72,000 troops at Waterloo were killed or wounded.

Pain in the behind

By the time of Waterloo, Napoleon suffered terribly from painful hemorrhoids. These made it uncomfortable for him to sit on a horse.

WANT MORE?

Find out more ☆ www.ngv.vic.gov.au/napoleon/facts-and-figures/did-you-know

CURIOUS CUSTOMS

Which country smashes dishes to see in the New Year?* Where would you find an ornamental green pickle placed last on a Christmas tree?* And what part of a bridegroom's clothing is cut to pieces during many Italian weddings?* All these and many, many more strange customs and traditions occur in different countries throughout Europe.

Cacti stand guard outside a Greek home.

Evil eye

Good and bad luck
The Irish Celts considered a four-leafed clover a lucky charm. Greeks place cacti near the front door to ward off bad things. For 3,000 years in Turkey, evil eye glass beads have decorated anything that may cause envy in others, from a new dress to a car. The aim is to ward off evil spirits.

A smashing time
In Germany, the night before a couple marry, friends turn up with plates, cups and other goods. They smash the items to bring good luck to the marriage. This is called *Polterabend*. The couple are left to clean up the mess!

WHAT THE DEVIL'S THE CORRECT TIME?

CLOCK WISE

Most churches in Malta have two clocks but set to different times. It's not a time zone thing. One clock tells the wrong time to confuse the devil, should he turn up.

*Answers: 1. Denmark 2. Germany 3. The bridegroom's tie.

Bad Santa
In Austria, Slovenia, and other parts of central Europe, Krampus is Santa's far-from-friendly alter ego. People go out wearing devil-like masks. They snarl and rattle chains to frighten children who have misbehaved before Christmas.

KEEP YOUR HAIR ON, DEAR!

CHRISTMAS CUSTOMS

Pooping log!
This is the name given to a Catalan custom in Spain. From December 8th, a hollowed-out log is "fed" with sweets, fruits, and nuts. It's then beaten with sticks on Christmas Eve or Day, so that the log poops out the treasures inside.

Spider inside
In the Ukraine, finding a spider's web on Christmas morning is said to bring good luck. So Ukrainians decorate their Christmas trees with fake webs and spiders.

WELCOME TO MY LUCKY WEB...

WANT MORE?

More customs ☆ **www.traditionscustoms.com/christmas-traditions/christmas-europe**

Flea

PLAGUE!

During the outbreak, it was known as the Great Pestilence or Great Plague.

The Black Death was the deadliest wave of disease to strike medieval Europe. It was a massive epidemic of the plague virus caused by bacteria carried by fleas that lived on rats. The outbreak is thought to have begun in Asia and been carried by traders to the Mediterranean. It reached Sicily in 1347 and, for six years, swept through Europe with devastating effects.

Durham
1349

London
1349

Paris
1348

Marseille
1347

Venice
1348

Constantinop
134

Rome
1348

Seville
1348

Sicily
1347

N

Yersinia Pestis virus

1000 AD

1345-1349

1500 AD

In London, England, it's still illegal for someone with the plague to take a taxi ride without telling the driver!

Way to go
Not everyone who caught the plague died, but those who did suffered horribly. Terrible fevers and pains in the back and limbs were often accompanied by large swellings all over their body. Dark purple or black blotches appeared on the skin from bleeding inside the body. Many victims seemed to go crazy or coughed up blood before dying.

GROSS!

Cities such as Paris, Hamburg, and Florence lost more than half of their people to the Black Death.

 outhern Russia
345

From Asia

2000 AD

Dim doctors
The disease and how it spread was not understood at all. In France, the Parisian Medical Faculty told people not to wash for fear that water would weaken their hearts! In reality, the filthy conditions found in many medieval towns helped the Black Death spread like wildfire.

Doctor death
Plague doctors tried to treat the sick. Some doctors wore heavy coats smeared in wax or raw sheep or beef fat. Their masks with long beaks were stuffed with straw, herbs, and scented flowers to ward off the stench of death.

BLACK DEATH TOLL:
at least
30 million

IT WASN'T ME.

OR ME . . .

GULP!

Dirty dogs
Dogs and cats were killed as many people thought they were spreading the disease. But this just removed many of the animals that would have preyed on the disease-spreading rats.

DOG 1355614

CAT 8167102

RAT 3690231

WANT MORE?

Some docs put live chickens on Black Death swellings to cure them—it didn't work!

ERUPTING EUROPE

It's AD 79. The 20,000 or so residents of the bustling Roman town of Pompeii (near Naples) were going about their business when disaster struck. Mount Vesuvius— a nearby volcano—began erupting. When Vesuvius blew, it blew big, spewing out over 1.4 million tons (1.3 million tonnes) of molten rock and ash every second for six of the most violent hours on Earth.

Archaeologists found the entire ancient Roman town of Pompeii perfectly preserved under the hardened ash layer.

BAD BOY
STROMBOLI

Excavation of Pompeii

FROZEN IN STONE

Pompeii and the neighboring town of Herculaneum were bombarded by the eruption. The towns were left covered in a layer of ash up to 82 ft (25 m) deep. Pompeii wasn't rediscovered for another 1,700 years, when it became an archaeological marvel.

Pompeii with
Mount Vesuvius
in the background.

Stromboli fires jets and fountains of red-hot molten rock from its lava-filled central crater. It's been doing this almost continuously for 2,000 years.

Home of Vulcan

Vesuvius, along with Etna and Stromboli, are Italy's three bad boys. They're all volcanoes that have erupted in the last century. Mount Etna is where the ancient Greeks believed their god of fire, Vulcan, lived. That's where we get the word volcano from.

Lava land

Apart from Italy, Europe's other volcanic hotspot is Iceland, home to 31 active volcanoes. In 2010, Eyjafjallajökull erupted big time, sending more than 305 million tons (300 million tonnes) of ash 5.5 mi (9 km) up into the atmosphere. The ash could clog up jet engines, so more than 100,000 flights had to be canceled.

5.5 mi (9 km)

305 million tons

TURN BACK!

Plaster casts were taken of some of Pompeii's victims.

Two of Pompeii's fallen figures

In a steam

It may be chilly outside, but bathers in Iceland's Blue Lagoon are toasty warm. This giant pool, not far from the capital, Reykjavik, is filled with piping-hot water heated by volcanic activity deep underground.

ANYONE SEEN MY SOAP?

Blue Lagoon, Iceland

WANT MORE?

Today, more than 2.5 million people visit Pompeii and all its exhibits each year.

I HAVE SO MANY MIRRORS, I CAN LOOK AT MYSELF ALL DAY!

On reflection
In the 17th century, you could own a mirror or a house but rarely both. That's how expensive mirrors were. Louis packed his monster-sized Hall of Mirrors, 240 ft (73 m) long, with giant chandeliers and more than 300 mirrors at eye-watering cost.

LIFE WITH LOUIS

Most European monarchs insisted on living in a grand pad to inspire awe amongst their subjects and envy amongst their rival rulers. Louis XIV (1638–1715) went further than most. He built a palace that almost bankrupted France. His father had shown few signs of grandeur beyond popularizing the wearing of wigs by men. But it was his hunting lodge at Versailles, a horse ride away from Paris, that formed the starting point.

Supersized Versailles
Louis gave his father's shabby chateau a chic and massive makeover. Around 36,000 workers and a big chunk of all of France's finances were poured into building the grandest palace in Europe.

GRAND GROUNDS

The gardens of Versailles are four times the size of Monaco. They contain 200,000 trees, 400 sculptures, a full-sized canal and vast fountains supplied by 22 mi (35 km) of water pipes.

x 200,000

 x 400

22 mi (35 km)
pipes

About 210,000 flowers and plants are planted in Versailles' gardens every year.

All about him
Louis adopted the Sun as his symbol, seen here on a fence at Versailles. He was known as the Sun King because it was said all of France revolved around him. Now that is self-centered!

PALACE TOP TRUMPS

ROOMS:	700
STAIRCASES:	67
FIREPLACES:	1,200
WINDOWS:	2,000
STABLES:	For more than 10,000 horses
COST:	Off the scale!

Causing a stink
For all his finery and etiquette, Louis stank. It's believed he only had three baths in his whole 76-year lifetime!

WANT MORE?

A fifth of the government's income went on running Versailles during Louis XIV's reign.

NO BUSINESS LIKE SNOW BUSINESS

Snow falls heavily in many parts of Europe so it's no surprise that people have always found ways to get around. Ancient skis dating back more than 5,000 years have been found in Norway, Russia, and Sweden. Skiing or skating for fun or sport is a more recent invention, as are some of these more peculiar winter pastimes.

Ski flying
Norwegian teenager Olaf Rye made the first-known ski jump in 1809. He covered a distance of 31 ft (9.5 m). Today's ski jumpers travel ten times that distance from giant ramps. Ski flying takes ski jumping to extremes. In Norway, in 2011, Johan Remen Evensen completed a whopping world record jump of 809 ft (246.5 m)—that's two and a half soccer fields long!

Slovenia's Robert Kranjec has made 140 jumps each more than 656 ft (200 m). That's serious ski flying!

SAIL AWAY

The Netherlands, Poland, Czech Republic, and many other parts of Europe have lots of lakes that freeze over in winter. These provide the perfect spot for ice yachts. These special yachts use skates or ski-like runners to skim across the ice, whipped along by the winter winds.

Ice yachts can top speeds of 62 mph (100 km/h).

Ice sailors wear life jackets... just in case they travel over thin ice and end up in water.

FLYING PAN

Wok racing? Yes, that's right. Kitchen woks with a reinforced bottom are sent hurtling down super-fast, ice-covered bobsled runs. Not on their own of course—that would be madness. Instead they carry a wok racer—a brave soul dressed in ice-hockey gear for protection.

In 2009 at the 4,265 ft (1,300 m) long Winterberg bobsled track, George Hackl hit 65.6 mph (105.4 km/h)—in a wok!

Check out those cooking ladles on his feet—they act as mini woks!

WANT MORE?

INDEX

NOT-FOR-PARENTS
EUROPE
EVERYTHING YOU EVER WANTED TO KNOW

1st Edition
Published September 2013

WELDONOWEN

Conceived by Weldon Owen in partnership with Lonely Planet
Produced by Weldon Owen Limited
An imprint of Red Lemon Press Limited
Northburgh House,
10 Northburgh Street
London, EC1V 0AT, UK
© 2013 Weldon Owen Limited

Project managed and commissioned by Dynamo Ltd
Project manager Alison Gadsby
Project editor Melanie Hibbert
Designer Clair Lansley
Picture researcher Sarah Ross
Indexer Marie Lorimer

Published by
Lonely Planet Publications Pty Ltd ABN 36 005 607 983
90 Maribyrnong St, Footscray, Victoria 3011, Australia

ISBN 978-1-74321-914-0

Printed and bound in China by 1010 Printing Int Ltd
9 8 7 6 5 4 3 2 1

www.redlemonpress.com

Red Lemon Press Limited is part of
the Bonnier Publishing Group
www.bonnierpublishing.com

Credits and acknowledgments
KEY – tl top left, tc top center, tr top right, cl center left, c center, cr center
right, bl bottom left, bc bottom center, br bottom right.

All images © Shutterstock except:
8br, 16tr, 28tr, 51cl, 55cr, 57br, 68bl **Alamy**; 12bc, 14tr, 16cl, 22tr, 30tr, 30bl,
31tr, 32tr, 33tr, 33cr, 33bl, 41br, 42t, 49tr, 53cl, 53cr, 61bl, 64tr, 65tc, 66bc,
67bl, 75br, 76tr, 76cl, 80bl, 82tr, 82br, 83br, 85tr, 92tl **Corbis**; 12tr, 12cl, 12br,
13tr **courtesy of The Ice Bar**; 44cl **courtesy of Legoland**; 8tr, 8cl, 9br, 10tr,
10cl, 11c, 13cl, 15tl, 17cl, 17br, 19cl, 22br, 24br, 26cr, 27br, 36tr, 37tr, 39bl,
44tr, 46tr, 46br, 47tr, 48c, 50tr, 50bl, 52bc, 55tr, 56cl, 58tr, 58c, 58br, 59br,
62cl, 64bl, 65bl, 70tr, 70cr, 71bl, 72t, 72bc, 74tr, 75bl, 78cr, 79bl, 79br, 81br,
93br **Getty Images**; 15bl, 69tr, 15tr **Rex Features.**

Cover illustrations by **Chris Corr**

All illustrations and maps © 2013 Weldon Owen Limited

> I HOPE YOU'VE ENJOYED THE GRAND TOUR.

LONELY PLANET OFFICES

Australia Head Office
Locked Bag 1, Footscray, Victoria 3011
Phone 03 8379 8000 Fax 03 8379 8111

USA
150 Linden St, Oakland, CA 94607
Phone 510 250 6400 Toll free 800 275 8555 Fax 510 893 8572

UK
Media Centre, 201 Wood Lane, London W12 7TQ
Phone 020 8433 1333 Fax 020 8702 0112

lonelyplanet.com/contact